NATIONAL PARKS

GLACIER
NATIONAL PARK

by Maddie Spalding

Content Consultant
Andrew G. Fountain, PhD
Departments of Geology and Geography
Portland State University

Core Library

An Imprint of Abdo Publishing
abdopublishing.com

abdopublishing.com

Published by Abdo Publishing, a division of ABDO, PO Box 398166, Minneapolis, Minnesota 55439. Copyright © 2017 by Abdo Consulting Group, Inc. International copyrights reserved in all countries. No part of this book may be reproduced in any form without written permission from the publisher. Core Library™ is a trademark and logo of Abdo Publishing.

Printed in the United States of America, North Mankato, Minnesota
072016
012017

**THIS BOOK CONTAINS
RECYCLED MATERIALS**

Cover Photo: Shutterstock Images
Interior Photos: Shutterstock Images, 1, 39; Jason Patrick Ross/Shutterstock Images, 4; Glacier National Park Service, 7, 45; Library of Congress, 10; Tim Rains/Glacier National Park Service, 12, 24, 37; Jacob W. Frank/Glacier National Park Service, 15, 18, 34; US Geological Survey, 17; Montana Fish, Wildlife, & Parks, 23; George Grantham Bain Collection/Library of Congress, 26; North Wind Picture Archives, 29; Rodman Wanamaker/Library of Congress, 32; National Park Service, 42–43

Editor: Mirella Miller
Series Designer: Ryan Gale

Publisher's Cataloging-in-Publication Data

Names: Spalding, Maddie, author.
Title: Glacier National Park / by Maddie Spalding.
Description: Minneapolis, MN : Abdo Publishing, 2017. | Series: National parks
    | Includes bibliographical references and index.
Identifiers: LCCN 2016945459 | ISBN 9781680784725 (lib. bdg.) |
    ISBN 9781680798579 (ebook)
Subjects: LCSH: Glacier National Park (Mont.)--Juvenile literature.
Classification: DDC 917.86/52--dc23
LC record available at http://lccn.loc.gov/2016945459

CONTENTS

THE CROWN OF THE CONTINENT

The Middle Fork Flathead River roars as it snakes through rocks. Its current pushes a sturdy raft. The ten people inside the raft brace themselves. Ahead of them, the river narrows. The water churns. Their guide shouts out a warning. The raft shoots through the rapid. Cold water splashes the group. They laugh and shout with delight. The water feels refreshing on the warm

The Middle Fork Flathead River is calm in some areas for more relaxed raft rides.

5

summer day. After a few seconds, the raft reaches calmer waters. The group looks around in awe at the sloping mountains and forests that make up Glacier National Park.

Glacier National Park is a wilderness landscape of forests, mountains, and lakes. It covers more than 1 million acres (405,000 ha). The park is located along the Rocky Mountains in the northwest corner of Montana. It is known for its snowcapped mountain peaks. Glaciers are found near the summits of some of these mountains. Glaciers are blocks of snow and ice. They can move

The snow at Glacier melts in the summer and flows into the park's many lakes and rivers.

through an area and shape its landscape. The park's name reflects the impact glaciers had in shaping this landscape. Ice near the surface of a glacier puts pressure on ice near the bottom. This allows glaciers to slide down mountains. Once a sheet of ice begins to move, it is called a glacier.

A Divided Land

Continental divides can be found in each of the world's seven continents. A continental divide is a ridge of elevated land that separates a continent's river systems. A river system is a group of rivers that drain into a larger body of water. The North American Continental Divide runs along the Rocky Mountains. It follows the crests of many mountain ranges in Glacier National Park. Weather along the North American Continental Divide can be unpredictable. Warm and wet air moves east from the Pacific Ocean. Cold and dry Arctic air moves in from the northeast. These two sources of air meet at the divide. This forms a unique weather system.

The west side of the park receives more precipitation than the east side. The east side of the park is drier and windier. Winds here sometimes reach 100 miles per hour (161 km/h). Blizzards form when moist Pacific air collides with the cold Arctic air. These storms can dump as much as 44 inches (112 cm) of snow on Glacier's mountains.

Taft's Decision

Glacier National Park is one of the top ten most-visited US national parks. More than 2 million visitors went in 2015. The area was also a popular destination before it became a park. The Great Northern Railway opened in 1891. Many people used this new transportation route to travel to Montana. Miners were tempted by the possibility of finding gold or copper. Hunters had heard there was a lot of wildlife to be found in the area. But many travelers

Grinnell admired Glacier's landscape and wildlife.

soon began to appreciate the land for its natural beauty. One such traveler was George Bird Grinnell.

Grinnell was a writer and editor for *Forest and Stream*, a sportsman's magazine. He visited northern Montana in the summer of 1885. He wrote about his observations for the *Century Magazine*. He called the area the "crown of the continent."

Grinnell wanted to protect northwest Montana's landscape. He approached James J. Hill with the idea of creating a national park. Hill was president of the Great Northern Railway Company. The company had built hotels in the area. Hill hoped the creation of a national park would draw in more tourists. Grinnell's writings and Hill's influence helped convince President William Howard Taft that the area needed to be protected. Taft signed a bill on May 11, 1910. This bill created Glacier National Park. Glacier became the country's tenth national park. Its natural beauty and distinct landscape set it apart from other places in North America.

EXPLORE ONLINE

Chapter One discusses why Glacier National Park was created. The website below goes into more depth about this topic. How is the information from the website the same as the information in Chapter One? What new information did you learn from the website?

Glacier National Park, Montana
mycorelibrary.com/glacier

CHAPTER TWO

GEOLOGICAL HISTORY

The Belt Sea covered present-day western Montana approximately 1.6 billion years ago. Wind eroded rocks and sand from the nearby highlands. Rain and streams swept these sediments into the Belt Sea. They built up on the seafloor until they formed layers of rocks. Magma from under Earth's crust later bubbled up to the surface as lava. This lava flowed onto the seafloor 750 million years

Natural forces such as weather, erosion, and glaciers created the landforms park visitors see today.

ago. It formed black rocks as it cooled.

The Belt Sea dried up more than 150 million years ago. But rocks that formed on the ancient seafloor are visible today. Other rocks are metamorphic rocks. These rocks were shaped by heat and pressure deep inside the planet.

Mountain Formation

Earth's surface is made up of land segments called plates. These plates are constantly moving at a slow rate. Sometimes they collide. When this

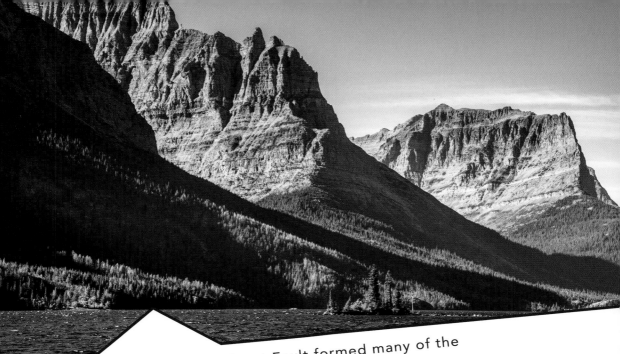

The Lewis Overthrust Fault formed many of the mountains seen in Glacier National Park.

happens, one of the plates may lift upward and form mountains.

The North American Plate collided with the Pacific Plate approximately 150 million years ago. Pressure built as the plates pushed against each other. Then a giant slab of rock broke free. This rock was at least 15,000 feet (4,600 m) thick. It slid eastward approximately 50 miles (80 km). It settled on top of younger rocks. Scientists now call this rock slab the Lewis Overthrust Fault.

Glacial Movement

The glaciers are around 6,000 to 8,000 years old. But glaciers actually began forming in the area approximately 2 million years ago. Earth went through a cooling period. Snow and ice built up on mountainsides and formed glaciers.

Ancient glaciers in present-day western Montana slid down mountain slopes. Some glaciers carved holes called depressions in

Glacial Decline

Scientists have documented glacial retreat in Glacier National Park since 1850. The image above compares the size of Chaney Glacier in 1850 to its size in 2005. Chaney Glacier is one of the 25 glaciers left in the park. How did the size of this glacier change between 1850 and 2005?

valleys. Rainwater pooled in these depressions. This is how lakes were formed.

Glacier National Park has 762 lakes. The largest is Lake McDonald. It stretches out from the park's southwestern edge. It is 9.4 miles (15 km) long and 1.5 miles (2.4 km) wide. Without glacial movement, none of the park's lakes would exist.

BIOLOGICAL HISTORY

Glacier National Park is known for its diverse plants and wildlife. Visitors may see bighorn sheep climbing mountain slopes. They may spot elk grazing on prairies in the east side of the park. They may also admire the fields of yellow glacier lilies in the meadows. These plants and animals can coexist here because of the unique landscape and climate.

A mule deer is seen along the shore of Lake McDonald.

Glacier's Plants

Glacier National Park is home to more than 1,000 species of plants. The oldest is the whitebark pine tree. Some of these trees have lived to be 700 years old. They grow on slopes at elevations of 6,000 to 9,000 feet (1,800 to 2,740 m). Whitebark pines are an important food source for many animals. Red squirrels gather whitebark pine cones and eat the seeds inside. Grizzly bears also eat these highly nutritious seeds. Whitebark pine branches often grow to be misshapen. This is because winds are strong at such high elevations. Wind speed sometimes reaches 100 miles per hour (161 km/h).

Whitebark pines are under threat. A fungus that causes white pine blister rust was accidentally introduced into North America in the early 1900s. This disease has killed approximately half of the park's whitebark pines. Many of the surviving trees are infected. But approximately 5 percent of these trees are resistant. They were exposed to the fungus but did not become infected. Scientists collected cones from these trees. They planted resistant seedlings. Their efforts have helped preserve this important tree species.

Western red cedar trees are also among the park's oldest plants. Some date back to the early 1500s. They thrive at lower elevations along with hemlocks and cottonwoods. These trees grow thick along park paths.

The park is home to many wildflowers too. These colorful

PERSPECTIVES
Naturalist Melissa Scott

Melissa Scott is a naturalist with Natural Habitat Adventures. She is also a nature and wildlife photographer with a special connection to Glacier National Park. Scott started working as a Glacier National Park guide in 1992. She was drawn to the natural beauty and began taking photographs of its landscapes. Her goal is to educate people about the park's stunning nature and wildlife. She hopes her photographs help people understand why wilderness conservation is important.

Grizzly Encounters

The first bear attacks in Glacier National Park occurred in 1967, more than 50 years after the park first opened. These attacks killed two people and inspired the best-selling book *Night of the Grizzlies* by Jack Olsen. These stories might scare park visitors. But bear attacks are rare. Bears are often attracted to garbage or food. Park staff advises visitors to keep their campsites clean and their food in hard-to-reach places. They also advise visitors to make noise while hiking. Noise scares bears away.

flowers bloom in meadows between the mountains. Glacier lilies are wildflowers. Another common wildflower is beargrass. Beargrass is not really a grass. It is a white flower. Bears use the leaves of these flowers as building material for their dens.

Glacier's Animals

Seventy-one mammal species live in Glacier National Park. Perhaps the most well-known is the grizzly bear. There are only approximately 1,800 grizzlies left in the lower 48 US states. Approximately 300 grizzlies live in Glacier. The meadows and forests are ideal for these bears.

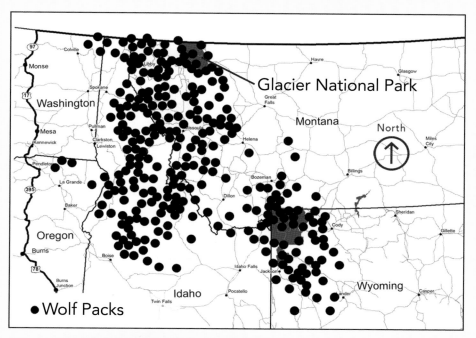

Montana's Gray Wolf Population

Many of Montana's gray wolves live in or near Glacier National Park. Gray wolves face habitat loss due to land development. They are protected in the Northern Rocky Mountains. The map shows the distribution of gray wolves in the northwestern United States. How can you tell from the map that many of Montana's gray wolves live in or near Glacier?

Other mammals include gray wolves and bighorn sheep. Gray wolves were heavily hunted in the mid-1930s. They were driven from their native habitats. Gray wolves from Canada crossed into Glacier National Park in 1979. The park became home to the first wolf den in the western United

Glacier National Park serves as an important protected environment for bighorn sheep.

States in more than 50 years. Since then the gray wolf population in Montana has grown steadily.

Bighorn sheep thrive in mountainous areas. But settlers took over some of their habitats in the 1900s. Their population shrank. Today there are fewer than 70,000 bighorn sheep in North America.

FURTHER EVIDENCE

Chapter Three introduced you to the animals and plants in Glacier National Park. What was one of the main points of this chapter? What evidence is included to support this point? Read the article at the website below. Does the information on the website support the main point of the chapter? Does it present new evidence?

The Wildlife of Glacier National Park

mycorelibrary.com/glacier

CHAPTER FOUR

A RICH HERITAGE

Montana is home to seven American Indian reservations. Two of these are located near Glacier National Park. The Blackfeet Indian Reservation sits along the east edge of the park. Approximately 10,000 people live on this reservation. Most are members of the Blackfeet Nation. The Flathead Indian Reservation is west of Glacier. This reservation is home to the Confederated Salish and

A Flathead Indian family celebrates a gathering outside Glacier in the early 1900s.

Going-to-the-Sun Road

Only a few miles of wagon roads cut through the park when it opened in 1910. Travel was slow. Early visitors had to hike or ride a horse through the rough terrain. The National Park Service decided to build a road. Workers started building the Going-to-the-Sun Road in 1921. Road construction through the high elevation was challenging. The 50-mile (80-km) road was completed in 1932. It was designated as a National Historic Landmark. This means it has historic significance to the park as well as to the United States.

the Kootenai Tribes. Approximately 5,000 American Indians live on this reservation.

American Indians once lived on the land that is now Glacier National Park. They have a long history here. The first inhabitants of northwest Montana arrived in the area approximately 10,000 years ago. Archaeologists have found spearheads that date back to this time period. These people were likely ancestors of the tribes that live near Glacier today.

Trappers were eager to explore the northwestern United States and find beavers.

European Arrivals

The first Europeans to come to northwest Montana were fur trappers. They arrived in the early 1800s. They were part of the Hudson's Bay Company. Hudson's Bay trappers killed beavers for their fur. Beaver pelts were in high demand in Europe. They were used to make hats.

Fur trappers encountered three groups living in the area. Blackfeet Indians lived in vast prairies

Kootenai Tradition

Apgar Campground is on the southeast edge of Glacier National Park. Settlers named this area in 1900. Before then, the Kootenai called it "Ya-kit Haqwilnamki." This means "The Place Where They Dance." The Kootenai believe that a spirit first taught the tribe its traditional songs here. Each song honors a part of nature or the landscape. The Kootenai have a spiritual connection to the land. Their ancestors came to the area every winter to celebrate a new life cycle. They danced for health and for spiritual guidance. Today a waterfall near the campground is named "Sacred Dancing Cascade." It honors the Kootenai's connection to the area.

east of the Rocky Mountains. Salish and Kootenai Indians lived in the western valleys. Fur trappers gave items such as guns and blankets to the Blackfeet. In return the Blackfeet hunted beavers for the trappers.

European fur trappers carried diseases into the area. The most deadly was smallpox. Thousands of American Indians died from this disease. More settlers arrived in the late 1800s. The last stretch of the Great Northern Railway was built into northwest Montana.

Settlers began establishing small towns in the valleys. Miners also flocked to the area. They came in search of gold and copper.

From Mining Settlement to National Park

Settlers hunted buffalo into near extinction by 1895. The Blackfeet had relied on buffalo as a main food source. Many people faced starvation. Only approximately 1,000 Blackfeet still lived in the area. The federal government wanted to purchase part of their lands to expand mining activity. The Blackfeet sold more than 800,000 acres (324,000 ha) to the government.

The Montana mining boom only lasted a few years. Miners were unable to find much copper or gold. The land the government had bought from the Blackfeet was slowly abandoned. Writer and conservationist George Bird Grinnell persuaded the Forestry Commission to designate this land as a forest reserve in 1896. Animals and plants in reserves were

The Blackfeet sold their land because they needed money for food and supplies.

given special protection. Then Grinnell fought for the creation of a national park.

President Taft signed the bill creating Glacier National Park in 1910. The park was further expanded in 1932. President Herbert Hoover and R. B. Bennett, Canada's prime minister, signed bills that created Waterton-Glacier International Peace Park. Both US and Canadian park officials maintain Waterton-Glacier International Peace Park.

Grinnell fought many years for the creation of a national park in northwest Montana. He described the landscape in his 1901 essay "The Crown of the Continent":

> Far away in northwestern Montana, hidden from view by clustering mountain-peaks, lies an unmapped corner— the Crown of the Continent. The water from the crusted snowdrift which caps the peak of a lofty mountain there trickles into tiny rills, which hurry along north, south, east, and west, and growing to rivers, at last pour their currents into three seas. From this mountain-peak the Pacific and the Arctic oceans and the Gulf of Mexico receive each its tribute.
>
> Here is a land of striking scenery. . . . No words can describe the grandeur and majesty of these mountains, and even photographs seem hopelessly to dwarf and belittle the most impressive peaks.
>
> Source: George Bird Grinnell. "The Crown of the Continent." UNZ.org. UNZ.org, n.d. Web. Accessed June 3, 2016.

Consider Your Audience

Adapt this passage for a different audience, such as a teacher or a friend. Write a blog post conveying this same information for the new audience. How does your post differ from the original text and why?

GLACIER NATIONAL PARK TODAY

Visitors to Glacier National Park today can see the way glaciers shaped the landscape. They can go on nature walks to view the many plants and animals. The Museum of the Plains Indians offers information about Glacier's American Indian history. All of this rich history made Glacier into the park it is today.

Glacier offers activities to fit all preferences.

Park Attractions

People from around the world visit Glacier. Some prefer low-key activities such as nature walks. Others prefer more adventurous activities such as horseback riding.

An area called Many Glacier is one of the most popular locations. It is in the heart of the park. A large number of glaciers are clustered here. Hiking trails wind through mountains. Hikers can make the trek to nearby Grinnell Glacier. Those who prefer exploring lakes can go on boat tours. These are offered at Grinnell Lake

Native America Speaks

Glacier National Park launched the Native America Speaks program in 1984. This annual summer program allows visitors to learn about the history, culture, and tradition of American Indian people who live nearby. American Indian speakers teach visitors tribal history and tell them traditional stories. Artists demonstrate tribal songs and dances. This program helps visitors appreciate the rich and diverse native history of the region.

Trails in Lake McDonald Valley lead to waterfalls and other nearby lakes.

and other lakes in Many Glacier. Tour guides also offer horseback rides along the trails.

Lake McDonald Valley is a popular attraction on the west side of the park. This valley contains Lake McDonald, the largest lake in the park. Campers have access to four campground sites around the lake. Visitors can explore the trails on foot or on horseback.

Logan Pass is a must-see driving destination. This is the highest elevation reachable by car. Located at 6,640 feet (2,024 m), this mountain pass is accessible from Going-to-the-Sun Road. Colorful wildflowers bloom here in the summer. Visitors hiking along trails at Logan Pass may see mountain goats or bighorn sheep.

Conservation Efforts

Tribal groups around Glacier play a vital role in preserving the park. Their efforts have kept oil and gas companies from drilling near the park. Some companies had been fighting to drill in the

Glacier is the Blackfeet's ancestral homeland, and they fight tirelessly to protect it.

Badger-Two Medicine region for more than 30 years. But the Blackfeet people fought back.

The Badger-Two Medicine region lies along the southeast border of Glacier, between the park and the Blackfeet Indian Reservation. This area has special significance for the Blackfeet people. But the federal government began issuing leases in the Badger-Two Medicine area to oil and gas companies in 1982. These leases gave the companies permission to drill in the area.

Protecting Tribal Homeland

Kendall Edmo is a member of the Blackfeet tribe. She works with the National Parks Conservation Association. She lives on the Blackfeet Reservation. She did not develop a strong interest in her tribe's language or tradition until after she completed college and returned to the reservation. Since then she has fought for the preservation of Badger-Two Medicine:

> *Our cultural connection to this land is deeper than us just occupying it. It's a vital connection to our identity. . . . The Badger-Two Medicine reminds us of who we are and who we were.*

The government later ruled that these leases were illegal. The Blackfeet urged the government to cancel the remaining leases. Their efforts paid off in 2016. The federal government recognized Badger-Two Medicine as a sacred area that should not be drilled. The Blackfeet succeeded in protecting both their homeland and Glacier National Park. Their conservation efforts will continue to preserve the park for years to come.

Chief Earl Old Person is a leader of the Blackfeet tribe. He wrote a letter to President Barack Obama in March 2015. In his letter, he urged Obama to help end the remaining oil company leases on the Badger-Two Medicine area:

> The Badger-Two Medicine for thousands of years has helped shape the identity of the Blackfeet people. This area has been utilized as a sanctuary for not only the wildlife, but also for our people to come together and realize their spirituality and to be in touch with their creator. . . . These ancient lands are among the most revered landscapes in North America and [they] should not be sacrificed for any price. I believe that your Administration has the authority, the foresight, and the principle to cancel these remaining leases, and to permanently protect the integrity of our cultural and natural heritage.

> Source: Chief Earl Old Person. "Letter to President Barack Obama." Badger-Two Medicine. The Blackfeet Nation, March 19, 2015. Web. Accessed April 8, 2016.

What's the Big Idea?

Take a close look at this passage. How does Chief Old Person try to convince President Obama to save Badger-Two Medicine? What language does he use? How does he explain the area's significance to both the Blackfeet and the general public?

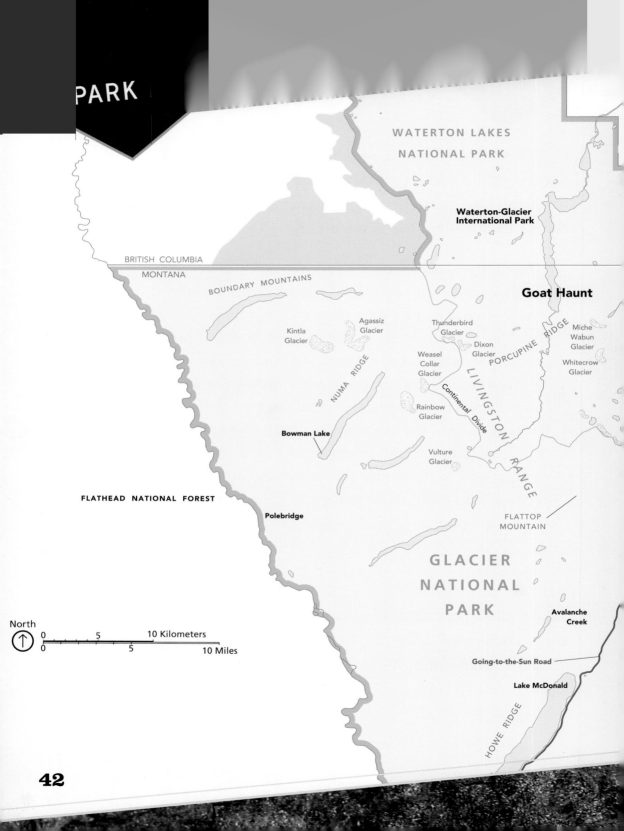

PARK

WATERTON LAKES
NATIONAL PARK

**Waterton-Glacier
International Park**

BRITISH COLUMBIA
MONTANA

BOUNDARY MOUNTAINS

Goat Haunt

Kintla
Glacier

Agassiz
Glacier

Thunderbird
Glacier

Dixon
Glacier

Miche
Wabun
Glacier

PORCUPINE RIDGE

Weasel
Collar
Glacier

Whitecrow
Glacier

NUMA RIDGE

Continental Divide

LIVINGSTON RANGE

Rainbow
Glacier

Bowman Lake

Vulture
Glacier

FLATHEAD NATIONAL FOREST

Polebridge

FLATTOP
MOUNTAIN

GLACIER
NATIONAL
PARK

**Avalanche
Creek**

North

0   5   10 Kilometers
0   5   10 Miles

Going-to-the-Sun Road

Lake McDonald

HOWE RIDGE

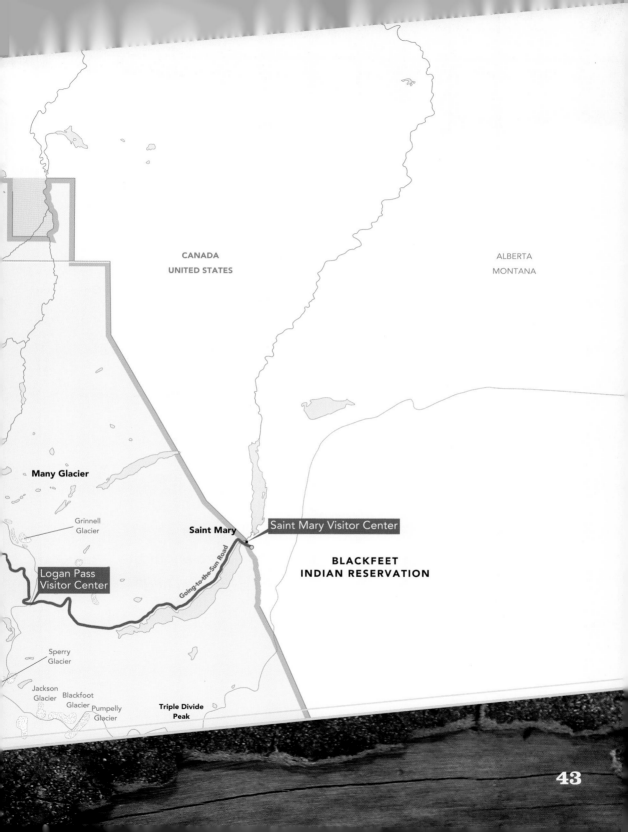

CANADA
UNITED STATES

ALBERTA
MONTANA

Many Glacier

Grinnell
Glacier

Saint Mary

Saint Mary Visitor Center

Logan Pass
Visitor Center

Going-to-the-Sun Road

BLACKFEET
INDIAN RESERVATION

Sperry
Glacier

Jackson
Glacier   Blackfoot
           Glacier   Pumpelly
                      Glacier

Triple Divide
Peak

STOP AND THINK

Tell the Tale

Chapter Five of this book describes some of the activities visitors can do in Glacier National Park. Imagine you are doing one of these activities. Write 200 words about the plants and animals you encounter. How might the plants and animals you see in one part of the park be different than the plants and animals you would see in another part?

You Are There

This book discusses early settlements in northwest Montana. Imagine you are among the first people to settle there. Write a letter home telling your friends what you have found. What do you notice about the landscape? What plants and animals can you find? Be sure to add plenty of details to your notes.

Say What?

Studying a national park can mean learning a lot of new vocabulary. Find five words in this book you've never heard before. Use a dictionary to find out what they mean. Then write the meanings in your own words, and use each word in a new sentence.

Dig Deeper

After reading this book, what questions do you still have about Glacier National Park? With an adult's help, find a few reliable sources that can help you answer your questions. Write a paragraph about what you learned.

GLOSSARY

archaeologist
a person who studies the bones and tools of ancient people to learn about the past

climate change
a long-term change in Earth's climate, including temperature and weather conditions

conservation
the protection of animals, plants, and natural resources

extinction
a situation that occurs when a species dies out completely

magma
melted rock beneath Earth's surface

naturalist
someone who studies animals and plants

pelt
an animal's skin with the hair or fur still on it

reservation
an area of land set aside by the government for a specific purpose

reserve
an area of land where animals and plants are given special protection

sediments
rock, sand, or dirt that has been carried to a place by water, wind, or a glacier

seedlings
young plants that have been grown from seeds

LEARN MORE

Books

Bjorklund, Ruth. *Montana*. New York: Cavendish Square, 2016.

Graf, Mike. *Going to the Sun: Glacier National Park*. Guilford, CT: FalconGuides, 2012.

Tieck, Sarah. *Blackfoot*. Minneapolis, MN: Abdo, 2015.

Websites

To learn more about National Parks, visit **booklinks.abdopublishing.com**. These links are routinely monitored and updated to provide the most current information available.

Visit **mycorelibrary.com** for free additional tools for teachers and students.

INDEX

ABOUT THE AUTHOR

Maddie Spalding is a writer from Minnesota. She enjoys writing about history and the environment. She has visited a few US national parks and hopes to visit more in the future.